Does Feminism Support Infidelity?

Does Feminism Support Infidelity?

THROUGH THE NOVELS OF MANJU KAPUR WITH SPECIAL EMPHASIS ON HOME AND A MARRIED WOMAN

Dhanya Panicker

SMART MOVES PUBLICATION E-5/11 Above Woodland Showroom, Bitten Market Bhopal -462038 (M.P.) India, USA Email :- isbn@smartmovesonline.org www.smartmovesonline.or

Contents

Book Title: Does Feminism Support Infidelity? Through The Novels of Manju Kapur with Special Emphasis on Home and a Married Woman

Book Author: Dhanya Panicker
Published by SMART MOVES
E 5/11, 2nd Floor, Bitten Market
Bhopal-462038
India

Printed and bound by SMART MOVES
E 5/11, 2nd Floor, Bitten Market
Bhopal-462038
India
p-ISBN: " 978-81-940996-8-0"
e-ISBN : " 978-81-940996-9-7 "

This edition published in: 2019 ISBN (ISBN Pending)
Copyright ©2019 by Dhanya Panicker

Dhanya Panicker, asserts the moral right to be identified as the author of this work.

This book is a work of fiction and any resemblance to actual persons, living or dead, events and locales is purely coincidental.

SMART MOVES

India. USA.

p-ISBN 978-81-940996-8-0

e-ISBN: 978-81-940996-9-7

Preface

Right from the beginning of the feminist movement, the problems faced by woman in a patriarchal world, her endurance and self sacrificing nature are widely discussed. But how women should shatter these manacles of indifference created by a male dominated society is less dealt with. At the outset, we can see many feminist novels depicting the life of women in home and society as a derogatory being. Woman was portrayed as the one who tolerates every pain- both mental and physical without any complaints. Many writers made this suffering as the central theme of their novels. Search for identity became the central theme of many Indian feminist novels. But when the theme of protest emerged, writers began to fortify the theme by introducing the theme of infedility supporting feminism. Manju Kapur, a blooming writer, responds in a quite different manner in such a situation. This difference in her thoughts makes her writing unique. She does not want women always endure all the troubles imposed on them by patriarchy. All her protagonists are educated. Through them she raises her voice against gender discrimination and other social evils prevailing in a male dominated society. She creates the concept of New Women in them. A new woman, who transgress the limits of Indian culture and the one who fights for her noble rights- both the types are portratyed in her novels. This book aims to discuss the women question still prevalent in Indian society and how differently Traditional Indian women and New Indian women in Manju Kapur's novels respond to each situation. Manju Kapur is a writer who aims her characters to follow Indian culture. She aims at creating a New Woman who is both feminine as well as strong. This is the woman whom India needs. Taking the characters in all her five novels, we can find that the strong woman who follows Indian culture could find satisfaction in her life. But the woman who transgressed the limits had to pay for her actions. The New Indian woman in all her novels, with special reference to *Home* and *A Married Woman* is discussed in detail.

Introduction: Manju Kapur

An internationally acclaimed Indian woman novelist, Manju Kapur, the Common Wealth Prize winner is also called the Jane Austen of India. Born on 6th August 1948 in Amritsar, she has lived through the turbulent times in India. She was graduated from the Miranda House University College for Women. Then she took her MA at Dalhousie University in Halifax in Nova Scotia and an M.Phil from Delhi University. She then returned to her alma mater Miranda House as a teacher and retired from there. As her father worked in the cultural attaché in the Indian Embassy in America and Canada, she spent her childhood there. She is married to Gun Nidhi Dalmia, and has three children. She lives in Delhi.

She is one of the famous post independence feminist writers who fought for the rights of women through her novels. She has written five full length novels. *Difficult Daughters* (1998), *A Married Woman (2002), Home (2006), The Immigrant (2009) and Custody (2011)* are her widely acclaimed novels. All her novels deal with the problems faced by Indian woman in her life and how she deals with these problems. Her debut novel *Difficult Daughters* won the Commonwealth Prize for First Novels (Eurasia Section) and became a best seller in India. *Home* was shortlisted for Hutch Crossword Book award.

Many customs like Purdah system, child marriage, Sati, ban on remarriage etc prevailed in India and all these customs marginalized women. The feminists united to eradicate these social evils from our society. Preserving the culture of India, Manju Kapur wanted her characters to be strong enough to gain their genuine rights which society once denied. She is a post colonial feminist writer who raised her voice against the traditional patriarchal culture. She is the one who introduced the concept of 'New Woman' in Indian novels. Till then, the Indian feminist writers dealt with the pathetic condition Indian women suffered in this male dominated society. Manju Kapur wanted her protagonists to move a step forward from these woman stereotypes. She wanted a woman who questions the rules regulated by patriarchy and who breaks all the shackles which limits her from gaining an identity of her own. Though she craves for gender equality in all aspects, she never wants her characters, especially her women characters to move away from the culture of their mother country. There is an underlying moral in all her novels. She never wants her feminism to go beyond the limits of Indian culture.

In Vedic religion, women were given the status of goddesses and it is believed that from their *Shakthi* emanated the male strength. The Vedas emphasized that women enjoyed a reasonably high position during the Vedic period. Two great epics of Hinduism, namely, *Ramayana* and *Mahabharatha* portray women in a good light. In Indian culture, the word which denotes strength and power is feminine, that is, *Shakthi,* and all male power is derived from this feminine. Then why she degrades herself by being a puppet in the hands of other men or engaging herself in activities beyond our culture.

Kapur wants a new woman who should also be a role model for all others. A new woman which suits India. By being strong, she should never move away from her character. Cherishing the beauty and purity of her character, she should be strong enough to face the problems in her life. She should be chaste, never be spoilt. By seeking pleasure in extra marital relationships, women are proving themselves weak as well as worthless. A strong woman should have the ability to stand alone. Through her novels, she portrays women from different generations and their character to state her view.

The language she used and the portrayal of her characters vividly depicts the clear picture of an Indian society and the situation Indian women had to face in the patriarchal society. She talks about the real Indian life and society, the roots of Indian psyche, family centered life, generation gap and all real life situations faced by common man.

Manju Kapur, the Common Wealth Prize recipient, is a celebrated Indian writer and enjoys a position of high esteem in the literary world. Her impeccable narratives of Indian domestic realities have earned her the title 'Jane Austen of India.'

1

Indian Feminism

Though India got her independence the women here are still given a derogatory status in the Indian society. She has little freedom of choice in the most consequential matters of her life like marriage, education and career. Though feminist activities reached its heights, she is still in the shackles of convention. Woman herself allows others to build a stone wall around her desires, not knowing what lies outside the wall. She never offers herself the chance to experience a life of liberty and equality, hence the wall of patriarchy becomes the mighty and the only truth she experiences in a life time. Who is there to question her rights unless she allows them to do so? It is her silence that gives them the green signal. 'Silence' is the symbol of endurance while 'Speech' signifies self expression and emancipation. Woman should speak out. She should fight to gain her rights. No external power can do this for her. It is the restricting thought that she is inferior to men, prevents her from doing so. Only the inner conscience in her is responsible for all her troubles. She should know her worth. It is she alone who has to awaken herself for a better tomorrow and a just society.

In a patriarchial society, right from the time of a girl child's birth, she is conditioned and constructed by the ideas of femininity. In this unequal and male oriented society women are moulded to suit the needs of men. They are forced to internalize the patriarchal culture and live accordingly as though they are created to obey and serve men. Their aptitudes have always been regarded as inferior to those of men. But this concept has undergone a sea change in the course of centuries. In our modern society women urge to be independent. The increasing number of educated females and the shattering of the meta narrative of 'the angel in the house' have given the Indian women the guts and voice to expose the long told lie of male superiority.

According to the norms of Indian society, women are always considered inferior to men. Indian tradition teaches women to defer to their husbands. She must always depend her husband for her needs. The male world imposes unlimited restrictions on women. Nobody was dared to question the norms followed in the name of patriarchy. Patriarchy and tradition always played the role of a villain in the life of a woman. Women were severely bound by cultural constraints and prejudices. They were not only restrained to remain at home, but also enforced and pressurized both emotionally and physically.

When a girl child is born, both the society and family pressurize her to perform all the domestic activities. Keeping her mother and grandmother as her role models, she should follow their path to respect and obey what patriarchy says. Devoid of education, she was taught all the house hold activities. A good training to become a perfect wife and mother is given to her by the elder female members of the family. In future she should be capable of taking the burden of the family on her shoulders.

Differentiation between the masculine and the feminine has always influenced all aspects of social relations. In real life situations, from time immemorial, we can see that patriarchy denied women's dignity and identity. Women were forced to fit their experience and expressions into the framework created by men.

Literature is considered as the mirror of life. As life itself is portrayed in literature, so is the condition of women. In literature too, women were pictured as passive listeners and like slaves to their husband and family. They were not allowed to raise their voice of protest.

After independence, the condition of the country changed, too changed the condition of women in India. From *Abala* to *Shakthi,* their position changed from homeward creatures to professionals. The works of Indian women writers had been undervalued earlier. This contempt too changed after independence. Literature in India too flourished. Women novelists began to transmit their experiences through their writings. A new dimension can be seen here. India has gifted several women writers with the talent of presenting a new version of Indian women and society within the limits of dignity and decency. Indian women writers began to focus on the suffering of frustrated Indian women. Their works present the problems faced by a middle class Indian society, mainly the women in those families, their struggle, suffering, identity crisis, protest and rebellion, man-woman relationship, alienation, child marriage and loneliness.

During the first phase, many writers merely talked about the frustration and suffering faced by women silently in their houses. In her novel, *The Nectar in the Sieve,* Kamala Markandeya depicted her heroine Rukmini, as a model of love, suffering and sacrifice, steeped in devotion and faith around the background of rural India. Different themes were dealt with in her novels. *The Nectar in the Sieve* (1954) dealt with the theme of hunger, while her next novel, *A Silence of Desire* (1960) on love and class conflict. *A Handful of Rice* (1966) is a novel on love and poverty. *The*

Coffer Dams (1969) is a novel on the predicament of migrants caused by dam construction, *The Nowhere Man* (1972) is the story of an immigrant Asian, *The Golden Honey Comb* (1977) on East- West dichotomy.

Shashi Deshpande's novels are concerned with the plight of modern Indian women, who are trying to understand themselves. She has a special interest in the destiny of Indian women and in their quest for freedom and identity. Her consciousness is dominantly, but not exclusively feminine. She has written a number of novels. *The Dark Hold No Terrors* (1980), *Roots and Shadow* (1983), *That Long Silence* (1988), *The Binding Vine* (1992), *A Matter of Time* (1998), *Small Remedies* (2000), *Moving On* (2004) are her widely read novels.

Bharathi Mukherjee's work focuses on the issue of migration, immigrants and feeling of alienation experienced by Indian women and their struggle. Her novels reflect the trauma of an uprooted identity. *The Tigers Daughter* (1971), *Wife* (1975), *Darkness* (1985) is a collection of short stories, the middleman and other stories (1988), *Jasmine* (1989), *The Holder of the World* (1993), *Leave It To Me* (1997), and *Kautilaya's Concept of Diplomacy* (1976).

Anita Desai is another celebrated Indian woman novelist. She holds a unique place among the novelists of India. She was short listed for Booker Prize thrice. Female characters play an important role in her novels. They are portrayed as rebels. Her novels present the agony of existence in a male dominated society. But her characters are sensitive and always struggle to make their married life a success. Her notable novels are *Cry, the Peacock* (1963), *Voices in the City* (1963), *Bye-Bye Blackbard* (1971), *Where shall We Go This Summer* (1975), *Fire on the Mountain* (1977), *Clear Light of Day* (1980), *The Village by the Sea* (1982), and the *Zigzag Way* (2004).

Another well known novelist belonging to this category is Nayantara

Sehgal. In contrast to Anita Desai's novels, Sehgal's novels don't depict happy married life. Deeply analyzing arranged marriages in India, she portrays a determined woman who is courageous enough to break away from unhappy marriages. Her female characters opt out of it and find fulfillment in extra marital relationships. Her major works are *A Time to be Happy* (1957), *The Time of Morning* (1965), *Storm in Chandigarh* (1969), *The Day in Shadow* (1971), *A New Situation in New Delhi* (1977) and *Rich Like Us* (1985) and *Non-Fiction Prison and Chocolate Cake* and *Far Fear Set Free*.

Kamala Das is another prominent English writer. Like her autobiography, My Story, her novels portray characters in search for identity and liberation. She has written her autobiography entitled *My Story* (1976) and two novels *Alphabet of Lust* (1980) and *Doll for the Child Prostitute*. The theme of most of her novels is protagonist's struggle for liberation and search for identity.

Another famous writer is Shobha De. In her novels, she studies about the marginalization of women in India. She is a very successful novelist. *Socialite Evening* (1989), *Starry Nights* (1991), *Sisters* (1992) *Strange Obsession* (1992), *Sultry Boys* (1994), and *Snapshots* (1995) are her famous novels. She attempts to shatter patriarchal hegemony.

Arundhati Roy, the other famous and renowned writer, essayist, activist. She is the author of the famous novel *The God of Small Things* (1997). She won the Man Booker Prize in 1997and Sydney Peace Prize 2004.

Manju Kapur is another notable novelist. She is a professor of English at Miranda House in Delhi. She speaks for middle class. A detailed analysis of all her five novels, with special reference to Home and A Married Woman is done in the following chapters. The theme of infidelity and how her characters end up are widely discussed.

2

The New Woman

An icon of changing gender norms, the *new woman* was the concept which rose into prominence during the late nineteenth century and has a profound influence on feminism. This was a term used to describe women who were fighting against the limitations which society imposed on women. Today a new woman may be called a liberated woman or a feminist.

The traditional Victorian society viewed woman as 'The Angel in the House'. This ideal of an angel was encapsulated beautifully in Coventry Patmore's poem 'The Angel in the House.' The poem describes the author's vision of femininity: a loving wife and mother devoted to her husband and children respectively. The life of women during the Victorian age was really pathetic. There was wide discrepancy between the rights enjoyed by men and women during that age. Women were seen as those belonging to the domestic sphere, providing their husbands with clean food and home and raise their children as society permits them to. They were mere properties to their husbands. Both single and married woman had to suffer hardships in the society. Most men viewed women as weak and incapable.

The Victorian *Fin de siècle* marked not only the end of an era but also a birth of a controversial figure, a new woman. "Free-spirited and independent, educated and uninterested in marriage and children, the figure of the New Woman threatened conventional ideas about ideal Victorian womanhood." (Greg Buzwell). The New Woman evoked fear in the minds of people in the Victorian era. In the words of Gail Finney, The New Woman typically values self-fulfillment and independence rather than the stereotypical feminine ideal of self-sacrifice; believes in legal and sexual equality ; often remains single because of the difficulty of combining such equality with marriage; is more open about her sexuality than the 'Old Woman'; is well-educated and reads a great deal; has a job; is athletic or otherwise physically vigorous and accordingly, prefers comfortable clothes (sometimes male attire) to traditional female grab.

Ibsen supported greater freedom for women and he expounded his ideas freely in his plays. The concept of New Woman was first introduced by Henrick Ibsen in his play *A Doll's House*.

3

Feminism and Infidelity

A bad marriage can possibly make a woman a feminist. The growth of feminism can be attributed to Western influence. Whenever we hear the word 'Feminism', we tend to remember Virginia Woolf, Simon de Beauvoir and other English writers. The growth of feminism is usually attributed to Western influence. Likewise, we possibly think of Radical feminism, which is the weapon of western feminists. But why don't we, especially Indians, think of a feminism which suits our country?

Indian culture gives more importance to society as compared to an individual importance seen in Western culture. However in Western culture society does not take part in the life of an individual. For the last few decades, Indian culture has been influenced by Western culture. But all movements are influenced by the culture of that country. Feminism is multicultural and diasporic. The needs of women living in different countries vary. Women are conditioned by several factors: familial, societal or racial, marital, economic, cultural etc. in such a diverse context, it would not be right to associate Indian feminism with the Western, as the Western feminism is usually marked by radical norms. Thus it will be awkward to ask the suggestion of Western feminist critics on the problems that Indian women confront.

Many writers have written about women seeking revenge through extra marital relations. Adopting the writings of many Western writers, Indian authors too have included the theme of infidelity in their writings. Feminism, especially Indian feminism, does not encourage infidelity. A woman is born strong, to face the challenges in her life. If she met with failures in her life, she should have the potential to stand alone. Extra marital relations are not a weapon of revenge. This makes one weaker and powerless. Women should be bold enough to face their own problems. Women, especially in India, are glorified as goddesses. Goddesses are bold and powerful. They are capable of facing any miseries in life. They don't need help from an outward source. Like Goddesses, she should not depend on other men or women to satisfy her needs. Goddesses represent motherly affection. They are symbols of chastity, love, power, beauty and other virtues. This is what Manju Kapur, tries to confirm in her novels.

New Woman in Indian Literature

A lot of changes have taken place in the socio cultural and ethical norms of the society. Over the past few years the status of woman in India has undergone a vast change. From merely a woman of household activities she emerged as a new powerful woman, who could easily handle both household activities and the duties of her profession.

Though the concept of New Woman was first emerged in England, in Indian literature, it was first introduced by Manju Kapur, the most distinguished feminist writer of Post-Colonial India. The Pre Independent Indian society was plagued by many social evils like Child marriage, dowry etc. Nobody was dared to question these anarchies prevailing in the society. Those who tried to eradicate them had met with strong resistance. The only solution for this never ending problem was that women herself should fight against these atrocities.

To know about their rights, women should know the world. For that she should gain education. She should feel herself safe in this society and she should be empowered to make her own decisions. Then only a woman with free spirit- a New Woman will be born. The new woman claims her individual worth and attempts to break through the suffering that traditional society offers her. The concept of the New Woman can be considered a by-product of feminism and the need of the hour for the Indian women. The New Woman is an empowered and alert woman who has all the qualifications- intellect, courage and skills- necessary to stand on par with any man and fight all inequalities. Through this she seeks a position of privilege, respect and freedom, which is her birth right.

Kapur moved a step forward from other Indian feminist writers who merely discussed the problems faced by Indian women in a patriarchal society. She wanted women to find solution for her own problems, the one who could create an identity of her own. Thus she created in her novels, a New Woman entirely different from the stereotyped traditional Indian woman who always remained a passive listener in her society. She knew that only through her writings she can urge women to fight for justice. The problems discussed in the novels are from real life situations so that women reading them could identify themselves in the place of the protagonists in the novels and would be able to take their rightful place in this world.

Kapur wanted her heroines to have identity of their own. As a teacher she desired that her heroines should be well educated. She knew that education is the weapon against all the prevailing injustice in society. Thus, being educated, women came to know about their roles in the society. They recognized their value and understood that both in family and society, they were as important as men were. They urged to create their own space there. They craved to enjoy equal status as those of men. Their education leads them to be independent in their thinking and use it as a tool against patriarchal rules and regulations.

Kapur brought her heroines to the forefront. She deconstructed the prevailing custom which marginalized women. She brought all her female characters to the centre by marginalizing male characters. She never wanted her heroines to be mere helpmates at home and hide their faces behind the doors. Instead she wanted them to participate in the discussions taking place in the family and speak for their rights. She portrays them in such a way that they were capable of taking their own decisions and questioning the rules imposed by patriarchy. Male hegemony is no longer welcomed. In her novels she mostly covers the picture of the life of modern woman in an urban society. Her novels deal with the issues faced by subjugated and marginalized women. The main problem she dealt with in her novels was the condition of women in contemporary India, the problems she dealt with and how she managed to tackle her problems in a male dominated society. her focus was on women and their problems. Her protagonists were all women and men had only the role of supporters. Her aim was to provide woman an identity of her own in her society. She should never feel herself inferior. She should know her potential and should gain her rights through rightful means. Thus Kapur drew the qualities of a new woman in all her novels. As a writer of India, Kapur never wanted to go beyond the culture and tradition of Indian society.

The new woman may be tortured and seduced, but she is conscious and confident. The trauma she faces may affect her mentally but like a phoenix, she emerges as a new woman. She gets rid of the position of the *other* and attains central position. She wants herself to be free from any restrictions imposed on her by the patriarchal society. She does not want to depend on her father, brother husband or son or any other male counterpart for her survival. Manju Kapur portrays this type of women who should be a role model for all other women.

Her debut novel *Difficult Daughters* draws the picture of Virmati, a woman who wanted to free herself from all social constraints. In the midst of household activities she craves for education. The novel depicts three generations of women quite different from one another in their thoughts and perception of the world. The first generation consists of Lajwanti, Kasturi(Virmati's mother), kishori Devi(Harish's mother) and Ganga(Harish's first wife). Their marriages can be dated back to the pre-independence era. These women seem to behave uniformly. They regard the institution of marriage as the be-all and end all of a woman's life. Here Ganga, Harish's wife was married to him during her childhood, she entered to her in-laws' house at the age of twelve. She proved herself as a good housewife but could never become an intellectual partner to her husband. Ganga is seen here as a victim of traditional society. From bondage to emancipation, the novel has portrayed the emergence of a new woman.

Kasturi, the woman belonging to old generation, is a woman stereotype, who lives under the rules and regulation created by patriarchy. She believed that a woman should always be subordinate to the male members of the family. She wanted to be a good wife to her husband and a good daughter in law to her in – laws. Virmati was her first daughter and as in the case of the first child, she was both a sister and mother to her younger siblings. Her mother took her caring nature for granted. She looks upon Virmati as a governess for her children. She did not want Virmati to concentrate on her studies.

Meanwhile, Virmati met Shakuntala, her cousin. She is highly influenced by Shakuntala's character. Her manners are royal and she has her own views of life and wishes to have a life of her own. Virmati decides to become like her cousin. It was Shakuntala who sowed the seeds of further education in the minds of Virmati. A professor of English named

Harish and family came to live as paying guest in Virmati's house. Ganga an uneducated lady is Harish's wife. It was during this time that Virmati's education was discontinued. The professor taught her English and asked her to continue her studies. After much toil, Virmati takes admission in AS College. Harish turns Virmati into an educated and enlightened girl. Virmati's tragic life starts here. She falls in love with Harish. Once she begins her journey towards her married lover, she doesn't even bother to establish an immoral and illicit relationship with him. The news about Ganga's pregnancy troubles Virmati. She decides to move to Lahore with her studies. But the thoughts about her lover haunt her in her dreams. Harish continues to visit Virmati in Lahore. Their relationship grows widely. She gets pregnant and she aborts the child by managing a gold bangle from her father. Harish only wants Virmati as his girl friend. He doesn't want to take the responsibility of the child or the abortion. After this depressing situation, Virmati ends her relationship with Harish. But Harish tries to win her confidence and writes letters to convince her.

He wins the game and starts meeting Virmati. After some months, Virmati goes to Siramur in Nahan, to become a principal in Pratibha Kanya Vidyalaya. Their meeting continues there too. They meet secretly in Virmati's room in the dark night. The news spread in the air and as the employee lost his trust in Virmati, she has to resign the job. She decides to go to Shantiniketan to forget Harish for her own good. But as she lacks concentration, she goes to Harish's friend's home in Delhi. Her dream of spiritual awakening and of renowned autonomy fades. She marries Harish and becomes his second wife. But as a second wife, Virmati was not allowed to do any household works or take care of her husband. Ganga was given the priority. Virmati's plight was so bad that even her parents didn't accept her marriage with a married man. In her husband's house, she gets only a marginal space. Harish too behaves in a passive manner. He turns deaf when she complains.

Her mother-in-law began to show her affection, when she becomes pregnant. But the care and love soon comes to an abrupt end when the pregnancy ends with a traumatic abortion. Virmati craves to become a mother but the fate denies. Harish's behavior with her is patronizing and domineering. It trapped Virmati. She no longer loves studying. She craved to see her parents. Harish sends Virmati to Lahore to do MA in Philosophy, which Virmati finds dull and meaningless. When she returns, she comes to know that all her family members have gone out because of communal tension. After some time, Virmati finds herself pregnant again. Finally, a baby girl is born and is named 'Bharathi'. But Harish rejects it and named the baby Ida.

Like her mother, Ida too turned a difficult daughter for her mother Virmati. Ida had her own dreams about her life. Ida gets annoyed and protests when Virmati asks her not to disappoint her father. Ida gets divorced after her marriage. Though she has pains inside, she is portrayed as a modern rebel woman who fights for her freedom.

A Married Woman is the second novel of Manju Kapur. The novel discusses the life of an educated girl born and brought up in a traditional family. Astha's father is a bureaucrat. He finds that his daughter possesses a lot of potentials and motivated her in her studies. But her mother wanted her to be a typical Indian girl, grown according to the rules of patriarchy. But Astha wants to continue with her studies. After her father's death, Astha misses him a lot. Her father used to take care of her education.

Meanwhile Astha falls in love with Bunty, an army cadet. At that time, Astha was at her teens. Astha is seen boasting to her friends about her relationship with Bunty. But the relationship ended when Astha's mother complained to Bunty's parents. Her second affair began with Rohan. Sometimes they cross their limits while playing with each other. But after a few months, Rohan departs to Oxford for further studies. This forces her to end the relationship with Rohan. Astha pours out her emotions in her daily diary. She wishes to become a teacher. But when she was doing her MA final year, a proposal from an MBA graduate from America came. His name was Hemant and he was an assistant manager in a bank in Delhi. Astha gets married to Hemant. During the initial days of marriage, Hemant seems to be an ideal and honest husband. But after few months, their married life began to show the sign of dullness. She took the job of a teacher and her in-laws too liked her decision. Happiness again returns to their life, Astha becomes pregnant and gives birth to a beautiful baby girl named Anuradha. After a few years, again Astha delivers a baby boy. Astha becomes busy with her children and job. Hemant too becomes busy as he starts a factory of his own. Astha complains as he talks only about his business, children and house. She finds relaxation by writing poetry.

A street theatre group comes to her school to hold a workshop. The group was run by Aijaz, a Muslim guy. He is a lecturer in History and organizes street plays to strengthen communal harmony in the country. He works for women's rights and praises them through his paintings and poetry. Astha feels that he is the only person who could understand her. astha comes to know that Aijaz is in love with a Brahmin girl named Pipeelika Trivedi. Astha wonders how Pipeelika manages to marry Aijaz despite everybody's objection. But one day Astha realizes that Aijaz is burnt alive in a van. Astha is now all alone. At that time she meets Pipeelika, Aijaz's widow and they became thick friends. Pipee criticizes Astha for being a traditional wife. But Astha explains her situation that she is the mother of two children who solely depends on her. Pipee becomes a source of solace in Astha's miseries. Astha finds a good partner in Pipee. As time passes, they engage in lesbian relationship. Meanwhile, Hemant doesn't like Astha's relationship with Pipee though he doesn't know about their lesbian relationship.

Moving away from social norms, Astha tried to create an identity of her own. But she reaches nowhere. Two women, Astha and Pipeelika ultimately compromise and find their own ways, knowing that they cannot have a future together. Pipee goes to US for her Ph.D. Astha becomes alienated again. But she gathers courage and goes to see her off at the airport. After seeing Pipeelika at the airport, Astha returns home. As she feels tired, she goes to sleep. Outwardly she looks the same, but mechanically, she has changed a lot.

The Sunday Times lauds her third novel *Home* as 'glistening with detail and emotional acuity' (Dawson, 173). In this novel she portrays both women – one with traditional views and the other, the most contemporary woman who raises the voice of protest and who wants to shape their destinies by assertiveness and self confidence. The latter is the woman whom India demands today- The New Woman.

Manju Kapur's *Home* is a great Indian family saga. It explores the complex nature of Indian joint family. The novel introduces the simple story of a joint middle class family 'Banwari Lals' which runs their cloth business in Delhi. Lala Banwari Lal is the head of the family. He has two sons, Yashpal and Pyarelal. Yashpal is married with Sona and Pyarelal with Susheela.

Sona and Rupa are sisters. Rupa is married to Premnath. Both sisters are childless. Rupa's marriage is an arranged one whereas Sona's is a love marriage. There are many instances in our society where a girl is accused of seducing a boy for marriage. Susheela is welcomed happily by the family as she brought a lot of dowry. Within a year, Susheela gives birth to a baby boy and when Pyarelal was 26, he became the father of another boy. The boys were named Ajay and Vijay respectively. Male child is given priority in the family.

Sunita, Banwari Lal's daughter is dead and their son Vicky is put on the lap of Sona, as she is childless. She takes care of Vicky as her own son. After two months, Sona finds herself pregnant after ten years. A baby girl is born to her and she is named Nisha. Vicky is now slightly rejected. The children grow. Sona gives birth to a baby boy. As giving birth to a baby boy is regarded as a blessing, Sona's mother-in-law begins to love her.

In a shocking situation, Vicky molests his cousin Nisha at the terrace while playing. Nisha, out of fear tells her aunt Rupa everything. She is taken to Rupa's house. It is pity that the little girl has to leave her home for safety and mental calm. Nisha is loved deeply in Rupa's home. She completes her schooling there.

Now she returns to Karol Bagh house. She takes admission in college and joins DBC with confidence. It's a new turn in Nisha's life. In the special bus for students, Nisha meets Suresh for the first time. They fall in love with each other. But once, Nisha's parents get a letter from the college authority informing on her attendance shortage. After this incident, Nisha is locked in the house. When enquired about the matter, Nisha doesn't tell anything directly to her parents. Instead she asks Suresh to meet his father. After inquiring everything, Yashpal, Nisha's father finds that Suresh is not of Nisha's type. Nisha has the urge to continue her studies. After three years of departure from Suresh, she has to think of another man as her life partner.

Her family wants Nisha to start her teaching profession. They find Nisha a manglik and they are searching for a partner. But Nisha leaves her teaching profession and starts a boutique. She feels quite satisfied with her new profession. Soon a manglik boy was found for Nisha. He is a widower but Nisha agrees to marry him. the novel ends with the naming ceremony of Nisha's twins. We can find a happy wife and mother in Nisha. She is enjoying her motherhood.

The Immigrant is the fourth novel of Manju Kapur. Man-woman relationship is the core of the novel. Another aspect of the novel is that it is set in a foreign country. The focus is shift to Canada instead of India. At the base level, the novel deals with the story of arranged marriage of Ananda and Nina but if we read the novel in the deeper level, we can find that the novel deals with more serious issues like search for identity, marital relation, adultery, clash between East and West culture. The life of an immigrant in an alien nation is well portrayed. It also portrays the problems faced by women in arranged marriage.

The novelist successfully handles the delicate issues of married life. The novel portrays the life of a couple whose married life is devastated by the sexual dysfunction of husband. It also focuses on the problems faced by a married Indian woman in an alien world. She also tries to save her married life. From the novel, we can see that the difficulties faced by a person in an alienated nation are nothing compared to the problems one faces in a married life.

The protagonist of the novel, Nina is at her thirties and is single. During her college days, Nina fell in love with Rahul. But he uses her for some time and moves on. In a country like India, marriage is the responsibility of parents. Nina is well aware of her parents' financial situation. An educated, ambitious woman, Nina is left alone with her mother.

At her thirties, Nina is married to Ananda, a dentist practising in Canada. She had to leave her mother and her job in Delhi to live with Ananda. She finds herself all alone after Ananda goes for his job. But Ananda doesn't worry about Nina being bored or lonely, because she has him. Ananda who is always under his sexual anxieties, has less time to think about his wife's situation.

Being unsatisfied with Ananda, the inner conflict arouses in Nina and she began to compare Ananda and Rahul. Rahul asked more about her satisfaction and how she felt when she was with him. After Ananda goes for work, Nina is left all alone in her house and she identifies herself as a lifelong immigrant. As days passed dispute between Ananda and Nina grew stronger. After much dilemma, Ananda goes for sexual therapy. With more confidence, he returns and hopes to have a better sexual relation with Nina, but fails utterly. Meanwhile, Nina visits the gynecologist and undergoes an entire checkup and finds that she is quite normal. It was Ananda who had problem.

In the mean time, Nina gets a job in the library. She becomes busy. Ananda starts illegitimate relationship with Mandy. He also feels free with Mandy while he seems to carry a lot of responsibilities while he is with Nina. Nina too, starts an illegitimate relation with Anton. She never feels guilty of her actions. After a while, Nina decides not to repeat her relationship with Anton and returns to India. But one day Anton arranges dinner for Nina and forces her to engage in sex with him. Nina is in search of love but everybody utilizes her for their own needs. She is not able to share her feelings with anybody and suffers mentally. At the end, we can identify Nina's life in Canada with one of a deprived immigrant.

Kapur successfully portrays the life of an immigrant – Nina, who had dreamt of a bright future with her husband, mother and child had to hear the sudden death of her mother who is in Delhi.

Kapur depicts extra marital relationships of these women protagonists. Nina had an extra marital relationship with Anton. Ananda, born and brought up in a Brahmin family, with set notions of morality, too involves relationship with white women when he came to Canada. Here Kapur has also shown how people enter into it and does not aim to pass any moral judgment. Nina's immigration struggles are well portrayed in this novel.

Custody is the latest novel of Manju Kapur. The main theme of the novel is divorce and its effect on the life of the divorcees and also their children. Disintegration of happy family and ugly battle of custody are the other themes of the novel. The feeling of unhappiness and conflict runs throughout the novel. Marriage in a joint family is portrayed in the novel. Children are the ones who suffer the most when their parents get divorced. The bitter realities of divorce are presented through the eyes of children.

Like the plot of her other novels, here also the story takes place in an upper middle class family. Here the very first scene is a love making

– but not between a husband and wife but between a wife and her husband's boss. The story revolves around two families. One is the family of Raman Kaushik and Shagun and the other Surya Kanth and Ishitha. Raman Kaushik, Shagun's husband, is a sales manager in cold drink company of Ashok Khanna. The work load for Raman was so hard that he could rarely see his wife. This created a huge gap between them. They have two children, Arjun and Roohi. Raman has very good relation with Mrs. Sabharwal, Shagun's mother. The first eleven years of their married life was quite normal. Later Ashok Khanna appears in the scene and his aim was to seduce Shagun. Mrs. Sabharwal felt something abnormal in the situation but she kept quiet and didn't want to teach her daughter morality, at this age.

The second is the family of Ishitha and Surya Kanth. Ishitha gets married to Surya Kanth. Due to her infertility, Ishitha was expelled from her husband's house. They get divorced. Ishiha's heartbreaks completely on the thought of being expelled from her husband's house, because of her infertility. Raman begins to doubt his wife whom he loves the most. On learning about Shagun's relationship with Ashok, Raman suffers a heart attack. Shagun decides to divorce Raman and responds to Ashok's relation. Although she is guilty, she decides to stay firm in her decision to spend the rest of her life with Ashok.Shagun asks for divorce by mutual consent. Though Raman first denies her wish, later he files the petition when Shagun takes their children with her.

Ishitha lives with her family in the same colony of Raman. Raman comes in contact with Ishitha. Ishitha involves herself in social work. Meanwhile Raman succeeds in bringing back his daughter Roohi from her mother. Fear fills Shagun's mind. But Raman is eagerly waiting for August 10, the date when the court announces its verdict.

Ishitha is interested in Roohi. As time progresses, Raman and Ishitha come closer. Roohi also loves Ishitha. Ishitha wants to adopt the child. Roohi likes to play with Ishitha. We can see a mother daughter bond between Ishitha and Roohi. Ishitha and Raman decide to marry. Ishitha now starts her life with Raman and Roohi. Ishitha's life is moulded into the role of a wife, mother and mistress in a large house with servants. Arjun becomes closer to his mother but not to his father or step father. He goes to US.

4

Conflict between Tradition and Modernity in Home

Home is the tale of a typical Indian joint family-The Banwari Lals.who aspires business with all its heart. The problems faced by women under patriarchy form the crux of the narrative, which unleashes before the readers in all its complexities. Gender discrimination is always a serious threat to equality. India has always remained a male dominated society where women and their potentials are suppressed in the name of tradition and culture. Hence the males get an upper hand in all matters- social, political, domestic and economic. The long history of India testifies female oppression by males. Contrary to this, in Manju Kapur's *Home,* the women folk are more exploited by members belonging to their own class that is, the women. Though quite shocking, this is a fact in Indian society-the women are more tortured by their loved ones. Thus the relationship between Maji and Sona, Sona and Nisha, Rupa and Sona are much discussed here. We find here that patriarchy is no more the monopoly of men, even women play their roles well. Thus a more complicated oppressive force is created here-the matriarchy. Kapur portrays the creation of matriarchy in a patriarchial society and the difficulties that ensue from this. As Banwari Lal and his sons are tied up in their business, much of the familial matters are controlled by women. The novel starts with the story of two sisters- Sona and Rupa and ends with the story of Nisha. Several woman questions prevailing in our society are discussed. The most popular one is the dowry system. Dowry system is the greatest curse of Indian society. Due to this evil system, the sacred bond of marriage paves the way to a business deal. There is a noticeable increase in the number of Indian brides documented to have died in their early married years under dubious and mysterious circumstances. The cause of death is constantly labelled as 'kitchen fires'. It is the most severe of all deaths because of insufficient dowry, by her husband or in-laws. The same issue is pictured through the life of Sunitha, Banwari Lal's daughter. Sunitha is married to Murali, a jobless man of irascible nature and who gives priority to dowry than his wife. He is an abusive ruffian and from the novel we can understand that he is the only person responsible for Sunitha's death.

But in the novel it is ironic that even though Maji knows how her daughter Sunitha suffers in her husband's house because of insufficient dowry, she still demands that her daughter in law should bring huge dowry. "The bride had to bring a dowry, come from the same background, and understand the value of togetherness. Falling in love was detrimental to these interests. How was it that their son, so sensible, had forgotten this?" (*Home*, 4) She even blames Sona that she might have done some black magic to entrap her son. Her second daughter- in- law brings a huge dowry according to her wish. These include a scooter, fridge, cooler, double bed and sofa. Sona now feels inferior to Susheela as her parents couldn't afford to give a dowry at the time of her marriage. The new couple starts living upstairs. Living upstairs was a wish for Sona, but as she came without dowry she was not allowed to live there. A girl without dowry is meant to do all house hold duties. Her wishes are not meant to be fulfilled.

Another issue in our society is infertility. After marriage, the girl who is incapable of giving birth to a child is always regarded as a bad omen in the society. She is labeled as "incomplete" or "worthless". The same is the case of Sona in the novel. After two years of marriage, she fails to give birth to a child. Her situation became worse when Susheela gave birth to a baby boy one year after the marriage. Her mother- in- law criticizes her occasionally, "What can you know of a mother's feelings? All you do is enjoy life, no children, no sorrow, only a husband to dance around you" (19). Thus Sona is marginalized by her mother-in-law. Marrying by love and not bringing dowry are enough for Maji to rebuke Sona, and above all, now she is infertile.

When her sister-in-law is murdered leaving her son behind her, he was brought to Delhi to stay in his mother's house. Everybody suggests Sona to become her nephew's mother. Nobody cares for the feelings of a childless woman. Even her mother-in-law doesn't try to understand her. She reiterates every day,"Beti, now you are his mother. God has rewarded your devotion. Sometimes our wishes are fulfilled in strange ways" (27). Thus, to fill the vacuum, Sona and Yashpal adopt the orphaned Vicky as their son. But Sona was not contented with the decision of adopting a child. She says, "A borrowed child? Ten years old? From another woman's womb?"(23). But as a loving wife, she pities the plight of Yashpal. "It was for his sake she wanted a child. He was such a good man, why should he be deprived of issue?"(24).

Rupa is very much affectionate to her sister. She too is issueless. But Rupa has accepted her situation. Sona says, "It is easy to accept when you have no in-laws always making you feel bad"(25). Rupa consoles her sister and advises her to consult a doctor and undergo a medical check-up. Being married to a rich family Sona "can afford the best medical care" (24).

In a male dominated society, we can see the practice of in-laws blaming the wife alone for the cause of barrenness. The husband may also be the reason behind it. A thorough medical check up is the only possible solution in this wretched situation. Rupa is confident that her sister will be blessed with a baby sooner or later. "One day your time will come, Didi, I am sure of it"(26).

After ten years of prayers and anxiousness, Sona gets pregnant. When she broke the news of her conception to Rupa, she too feels happy but suddenly the thought of her as the only childless woman in the family, disappointed her for a while. Sona gives all the credit of her pregnancy to Devi. "I feel it is because of the Devi. I felt a change after we went, didn't you?" (33). Rupa too felt her business had flourished after the trip. But the time she told Sona to go to the Devi of those hills again, Sona's attitude changes. She says sharply, "Your Jijaji can't be travelling all the time" (33). Here we can see Sona's real nature. She used to cry on Rupa's shoulders when she had no child. Only Rupa was there to understand her situation, console her, she was the only person Sona could open her mind with. But once things improved, she turned her back. Sona doesn't want Rupa to enjoy the pleasure of motherhood. Unlike Rupa, Sona is so selfish that she wanted to enjoy all the fortunes only by herself. She was just exploiting her sister's love for her own sake.

Next issue faced by women is gender discrimination and education of a female child. In olden days there was a practice of denying education to female child. Boys on the other hand were free to aspire education. Even they were allowed to go abroad and achieve education. This issue is also well represented in this novel through the characters of Sona, Rupa and Nisha. Sona and Rupa, the two sisters, are brought up in a middle class family. But they were provided education. Yashpal the shopkeeper falls ardently in love with Sona, and marries her threatening his family that he would otherwise accept celibacy. This occurred in a society which doesn't support love marriage. "Will Sona, from an educated family, be happy with shopkeepers? The boy is only high-school pass, but Sona now says she does not want to study any more, she wants to remain on the same level as her husband."(9)

The destiny of a woman lies in marriage. Even before Sona's parents could say anything, she herself steps out of the educational system. But Rupa was able to complete her degree uninterrupted. After her education, her father arranged her marriage to the son of a retired colleague. In Nisha's case, the irony is that Sona, her mother, who is from an educated family, even discourages her performance in studies. She passes most of the responsibilities of Raju, including his studies, on Nisha. She also gives her the caution that if she fails to help her brother in his studies, her studies too are not proved worthy. As a little girl, Nisha should give more importance to her studies. But her mother compels her to think of her future husband. Thus at the age of ten, she was insisted to keep fast for her future husband by doing Karva Chauth. Within a year after Nisha's birth, Sona delivers a son. The birth of the son is celebrated with great pomp and show. Sona feels that moment to be the most blessed in her life. Suddenly appears in her the attitude of indifference towards her daughter. Sona is not fit to be called an ideal mother. She shows gender discrimination between her two kids. She spends most of her time with Raju, the apple of her eye. She never gives Nisha the kind of motherly affection, love and care which a girl child requires most in her stages of development. Sona is unable to understand her daughter's feelings and expects her to follow tradition. For Sona, doing kitchen work is more significant than studies. When Nisha returns home after her cheerful days with her aunt and uncle, her mother began to crucify her. Sona finds out with horror that at the age of sixteen, Nisha's skill in cooking was negligible. "What can Rupa have been thinking of? I assumed she was teaching you everything she knew. You take half an hour to peel ten potatoes. How will you manage in your future home?"(126).

Today the most discussed woman question in our society is sexual exploitation of girls. The very same issue is exposed through the life of little Nisha. Nisha, a little girl of five year old is sexually exploited by her cousin Vicky, who is brought to Banwari Lal's house after his mother's death. Vicky, really the chip of the old block, like his father, doesn't value a woman's worth. He was so cruel to abuse a kid. Here we are forced to cogitate on the unique bond between mother and her female child, which is of much significance in feminism. A girl's closest confidant is her mother, whom she can trust everything with, whose presence always gives her a soothing effect from all strains of life. But poor Nisha, her mother, Sona always shows indifference to her. She gives much prominence to her son Raju. Nisha's bonding with her mother is lacking. Had Sona been more cautious about Nisha, she would not have been submitted to such a treacherous situation. Sona always insisted her to follow tradition. The greatest worth of a girl lies in remaining chaste till her marriage. To keep a girl virtuous in a society like ours, a mother should take keen interest in bringing up her daughter.

Home, where her mother is with her, the place of relaxation and comfort- all turns out to be the most insecure place for Nisha. She begins to have night mares. "In the nights to follow, the child's screaming became worse" (65). Later she is taken to her aunt's house and things change favourably. Nisha outshines in her studies.

Superstition is another issue haunting Indian society. When a girl child is born, the society is eager to know whether she is manglik or not. A manglik girl will bring ill luck to her bridegroom's parents. She might perhaps shorten her mother-in-law's life or bring bad health to her father-in-law. A boy born manglik is not regarded as a curse. His aim is only to suit a manglik girl. It is the only problem concerned with girls.

Nisha, the central character in our story too is a victim of this superstitious belief. She even suffers a lot in her younger ages only because of this curse. Even as a little girl, she had to take vrat.

Indian society is against the concept of love marriage. Sona – Yashpal marriage was also the result of their love. Their marriage was only given approval when Yashpal threatens that if he couldn't marry Sona, "he would devote himself to the life of an ascetic" (9). Only because it is a love marriage, Sona is from a middle class family and as her family cannot bear huge dowry, she was not given any value in her husband's house. Even her education didn't prove any worth. Same is the case of her daughter. As she loved a paswan, who is of inferior caste in the society, their marriage too was broken. When Sona discovers this relationship, she makes a lot of fuss about the matter. "This girl will be our death. My child, born after ten years tortures me like this. Thank God your grandfather is not alive. What face will I show upstairs? Vijay gets his wife from Fancy Furnishings while my daughter goes to the street for hers (198).

These are the main issues faced by women in a traditional Indian society. Through the character of Sona, who clings much to tradition, Manju kapur portrays a typical Indian woman who responds to all these issues in a passive manner believing that it is the woman's duty to suppress her feelings and be a good wife and good daughter-in-law in the society. Her lack of education, selfishness and narrow mind are well portrayed. Even as a mother, she couldn't play her role well. She was conditioned to meet the norms of Indian society. Simone de Beauvior's quote becomes relevant in this situation, "One is not born, but rather becomes, a woman" (vii)

The atmosphere, in which she lives, plays an important role in moulding her character. Sona is married to a traditional joint family, with traditional beliefs and values. There, women were considered subordinate to men and women's education secondary. The primary responsibility of a woman laid on her duty as a good wife and mother. Their place was considered to be behind the four walls of the house and their only job was confined to looking after the household affairs. Sona too tried to culturally condition her daughter to grow into an ideal feminine. But she failed to exert her plan.

Contrary to our traditional Indian woman Sona, Kapur introduces us to the idea of New Woman. Though most of us are familiar with this term, Manju Kapur gives a new outlook to this idea. Freedom is the watchword of the New Woman. The New Woman would not allow a domineering male, female or society to limit her opportunities. They are empowered woman who exercise control over their own lives, be it personal, social, or economic. They are free spirited, self reliant, educated and uninterested in marriage and children. Moving a little from this notion, Kapur's new woman is always emancipated but only within Indian socio cultural values. They too want to break the stereotypical notion of women who always submissively suffer the struggles imposed on them. They want to enjoy their human rights for liberty, equality, education, etc.

Manju Kapur portrays such a figure mainly through her characters Rupa and Nisha. Moving to Rupa, Sona's sister, we find her charater and ideas poles apart from that of her sister. The atmosphere in one lives, also plays a vital role in shaping one's identity. Though Rupa and Sona are born in the same family, their thoughts and life style changed after marriage. Sona breaks her education to remain the same level as her husband and had to switch over to the customs of the joint family. But Rupa attains her education and this helps her to think independently. She considers working woman as an emancipated individual. For this, she starts a business of pickles. From many incidents, unlike Sona, we find that Rupa never showed any discrimination between a boy and a girl. She always considered a female child to be 'Lakshmi' of the family. She gave importance to Nisha's education rather than her skill in house hold activities. She aims women's liberation through education. Rupa is not at all narrow minded and selfish like her sister. She considers Nisha as her own daughter and creates an atmosphere of love and care which Nisha lacks from her mother. Even Nisha's studies excel when she is with her aunt. It was Rupa's decision to send her for BA Honours. Rupa wishes Nisha to have a job and she should stand independently. Sona thinks a woman works only when there is no one to look after her. She asks, "What is the need to blacken your face looking for a job, as though you had no one to protect you?" Rupa always protests, "Times are different now, Didi. You mean to say all working women have no one to call their own?" But Sona defends saying, "We are old-fashioned people. Tradition is strong with us. So is duty"(124).

Now let's see how Nisha raises her voice against woman question echoed in her life. Nisha who finds her mentor and role model in Rupa, takes her as her torch bearer. She was always against the views and ideas of her mother. With great pain in her heart, Nisha finds that her mother always wanted her daughter to help her in the kitchen. When Sona criticizes her of not knowing any house hold works, she protests, "Masi said there is always time to learn cooking, but only one time to study" (126). She wants to progress in her studies. She too craved for woman's independence. As a child of ten years old, when Nisha was asked to do Karva Chauth for her future husband, she retorts saying, "Why should I? That's for older women." (93) She didn't want to spend the whole day fasting. She was against all superstitious beliefs. She wants to live like any other ordinary girls in her class. She wants only to be concentrated in her studies. Like a real New Woman in western ideas, she even declares, "I don't want to marry" (93).

When Suresh, her lover, approaches her with a false intention during an excursion, in the Vijay Nagar room, Nisha being a victim of this sinful act in her childhood days does not allow him to transgress the limits. She says to him, "It is just as well there is something left for when we are married" (192). Now she has become more cautious about her femininity. She doesn't want to be seen as a sex object. One day the relation between Nisha and Suresh comes to lime light. When Sona makes a great fuss on this topic, Nisha questions her mother, "You also did the same thing, Ma" (198). Here Nisha thinks quite differently. If her parents could do this, why couldn't she? She has to face much more criticism from others too. Her brother criticizes her that she is not trustworthy. Then she rebels, "Who are you to decide whether I am trustworthy?" (199). She doesn't want a man to question her identity. Here we find a new woman with modern perspective. Her family restricts her from going out or meet Suresh. Then her only ray of hope was her uncle and aunt. When her uncle tells her that it is the boy's family who should have met hers, she rectifies his traditional notion by saying that, "Uncle, this is the modern age" (202). Finally they meet him in a restaurant. Their meeting resulted in the destruction of her hope and love. After dreaming of Suresh as her husband for the past three years, Nisha has to adjust to the idea of another man in his place. At this point, Nisha's life started to move towards emancipation. Like her aunt Rupa, she too wanted to do something valuable. She successfully completed her degree she wants to do another course. "I want to study fashion designing. Why should I sit at home every day waiting for proposals?"(227). She wants to be economically independent.

The main woman question she had to face was gender discrimination. Even her mother didn't pay due attention to her only because she was a girl child. She no longer wants to be discriminated in the society. She determines to be independent like her brothers. For this she asks her father to help her to start her own business. Thus starts a new business in the form of a boutique named 'Nisha Creations'. It was the first time in her life she feels proud as her father trusted her as he would have trusted his sons. Her friends and customers like her dress and suits. She gets heavy orders and becomes a successful and renowned business woman of the market. She knows that only through economic emancipation, a woman could create a space in her society. She always keeps an eye on her workers. She doesn't want to spoil her name which she earned through her hard work. Here she fights the concept of gender discrimination by being economically emancipated.

Later she gets married to Arvind, a widower on the condition that she would continue with her business. There she had to face another trouble from her mother-in-law, who demands her daughter-in-law's presence all time around her. Thus she is caged like a bird. So she had to transfer her business to Pooja, her sister-in-law. But she decides to restart it after a break. Within a month of her marriage she conceives. She gives birth to twins- one boy and a girl. More than an entrepreneur, she is now a mother- a mother of two kids. She gives importance to both her kids, without any discrimination. Bound up in the duties of a mother, she spends more time with her husband and children. This does not mean that she is no longer an independent woman. She has proved her talent in business and studies, facing many challenges in life. Using the tool of education, Manju Kapur awakens her protagonists. Education helps one to think independently. In the first part of the novel, Nisha experiences a lot of issues which hurt her mind severely. Sexual assault and gender descrimination were bitter experiences in her childhood. Later in life, Nisha becomes self-reliant. Like her aunt, Nisha too craved for her education. Thus Nisha could create a space for herself and she no longer wants to be treated as a puppet in the hands of patriarchial conventions. She wishes to stamp her own identity in the society. For this she defies the social structure and gives a new definition to womanhood which suits her aspirations. In contrast to her mother, Nisha raises the voice of protest against the woman question. We can see her blooming into a successful business woman. Rupa, her aunt always supports her to become a woman with high willpower. As an educated and independent woman, she was free from the question of dowry. Though she had to discontinue her business for a while, she has already showed a flair for it. Inspite of facing many obstacles, she excelled in her life worthy of being called, "New Woman." Nisha's achievements proved to be app laudable when we look at them against the backdrop of social scenario of that time. She is a New Woman whom India dreams of.

5

Conflict between Self and Society in a Married Woman

A Married Woman is the story of a woman who was born in a traditional Indian family. Her mother who blindly follows the rules of patriarchy wanted her daughter to follow the same. She wanted her daughter to adjust herself with any situation she has to face when she goes to her in-laws' house. The novel portrays how Astha the heroine of the novel fights against this age old tradition and find a free spirited life in a male dominated society.

Through her protagonist Astha, Manju Kapur portrays her concept of a woman.

"A woman should be aware, self-control, strong will, self reliant and rational, having faith in the inner strength of womanhood. A meaning-

40

ful change can be brought only from within by being free in the deeper psychic sense"

Astha is an educated, upper middle class, working woman who was born and brought up in an urban society in New Delhi. Being a single daughter, Astha was her parents' dream. Her character moulding, her education, her health, and marriage were her parents' burdens. Her parents were very much conscious of her marriage. She was their future and hope. Like all Indian mothers, Astha's mother gave more importance to her daughter's marriage. She wanted her daughter to get married to a good man. Her father also took great care of his daughter. He even slapped her once or twice to mould her according to his expectations. Kapur successfully portrays her heroine's emotions, "Tears surfaced, but she wouldn't act sorry, would rather die than show how unloved and misunderstood she felt." (2002, 3)

Astha had a purpose in her life. She knew very well about her parents' dreams. But more than being married and being a good wife and a mother, she dreamed of becoming an independent woman. She is portrayed as a strong independent woman who is in search of her identity against the existing patriarchal rules.

Like all teenage girls, Astha too dreamt of her marriage and her future husband. By the time she reached in her sixteen, like all other girls, she was well trained on the diet of "mushy novels and thoughts of marriage". (2002, 8). She often imagines herself in the strong embrace of a romantic and handsome young man. When Astha grew up, she had her own dreams and desires about her life partner. She wanted to choose him herself. Bunty, a handsome young soldier used to visit her house very often. Astha was infatuated by this handsome guy. Bunty began to appear in her dreams. Astha fell in love with Bunty. The very notion of 'love at first sight' tickled her heart and she penned her emotions and began to send letters to Bunty. They exchanged their feelings through letters. But the day her mother found out her daughter's secrets, everything came to an abrupt end. Astha with great annoyance understood that it was none other than her mother who sowed the seeds of discord in her relationship with Bunty. When Astha joined the college, her mother was urged to do the primary obligations of a parent towards her daughter. But parents have their own limitations. In her college, Astha fell in love with Rohan and they enjoy physical relationship. The relationship only lasted for a few days as Rohan moved to Oxford for further studies and Astha got married to Hemant. Soon after marriage she found her life in great dilemma.

Her marital life was not like the one which she dreamt of. Astha's life was a tug o' war between tradition and modernity. She was an upper middle class educated woman, though financially independent, she had to face the problems of adjustment between tradition and modernity. She wanted to be a liberated woman. Yearning to be an independent woman, she had her own ideas about her life.

She wanted to be different from the stereo typed woman whom Indian society praises for her silence. She desired to be treated as an independent strong woman by her husband. She wished to be respected and couldn't tolerate being a doormat. According to Kapur's opinion, wives in India, "have to dance all sorts of tunes of their husbands" (44). Within a month, Astha began to get bored with married life. As a dutiful wife, she had to wait patiently all day for her husband's arrival. As Manju Kapur puts it, "her future suddenly seemed very pedestrian" (47). She took up a teaching job in Delhi and enjoyed it very much. She felt herself independent and strong. But when she returned home after job, she had to wait very long for drawing her husband's attention to her. Her husband, being a male chauvinist, didn't want her wife to be independent and didn't want her talents to be accepted. He wanted his wife to be an "angel in the house."

The conflict grows in Astha. She couldn't tolerate Hemant's attitude towards her. She suffered from recurring migranes and then a growing distance from her husband. At home, Astha feels quite neglected and marginalized. Tension and loneliness was the only problem diagnosed with Astha. Lack of care and concern and feeling of distance from Hemant began to kill her from inside. Astha began to pour her feelings through her poems. Her poem "Changes" captures her pain, longing and determination. "I would never suffer again but no matter how many times I heave…"Being born and brought up in a patriarchal society, Hemant follows the conventions and wanted his wife to be quite submissive.

Once Astha got a chance to break the shackles which was once a hindrance to all her dreams, she felt herself a strong woman. Aijaz Khan was the one who helped her to find her inner self. She succeeded in this attempt when she took part in the workshop conducted in her school. Thus Astha became quite aware of the incidents which took place outside the four walls of her house. During her struggle to seek self identity, she could hope to intervene in the social activities of the time. She desires to actively participate in the public sphere. In a world where Hindus see Muslims as the 'other', Astha wished to reconstruct her religious views, thus viewing all religions from the same critical lens.

Astha wished to go to Ayodhya to protest against the demolition of Babri Masjid . but her wish was crushed into pieces by her mother –in – law, who was a staunch supporter of Hinduism and wanted her daughter in law too to follow the same. She insisted on the tolerance of Hinduism and also refused Astha's wish to actively participate in the discussion of an implied Hindu tolerance. Her encounter with Aijaz the Muslim, made her recognize the drawback of her family and their traditional attitude towards the issue.

But she decides to participate in the progressive work conducted by Aijaz on the Ram-Janmabhoomi-Babri Masjid conflict in Ayodhya. Thus Astha involves more and more in outside works. Astha is compelled to see herself in much more broader context than the well-defined limits of her home. Unfortunately, Aijaz and his troupe members are dragged and murdered while performing the play on Babri Masjid and Ram Janmabhoomi. This incident affected Astha and led her to emerge as a social activist and take part in rallies for justice inspite of her husband's resistance. She also engaged herself in the painting for an exhibition conducted in memory of The Street Theatre Group. As Astha became more involved in the social work, she couldn't pay attention to her homely affairs. She failed to maintain a balance between her work and home. This created tension in the mind of Hemant and out of anger he asks Astha to give up all those activities. But Astha refused Hemant's decision, as she knew that this was the only way to have her own identity, self-independence and self-fulfillment. Her thought is clarified by her words, "I want something of my own" (148). Her words, "I need more space" (156) give emphasis to her point. She even asked Hemant to give her the room, which belonged to Sangeetha, Hemant's sister. But Hemant refused her demand.

Astha always desired to have a space of her own. She also wanted to enjoy her life not only wthin the four walls of her life but also outside the house. She also decided to take part in the meeting conducted by Sampradayakta Mukti Munch to protest and condemn the decisions of building up the temple of Lord Rama at the place of Masjid outside Rashtrapati Bhavan. But her in- laws and her husband refused it. But ignoring them, Astha went to Ayodhya to deliver a speech on the public meeting, as decided by the Mukthi Manch. Now she has made up her mind to fight against the taboos of the patriarchal society.

In Ayodhya, she meets Pepeelika, the wife of Aijaz. She feels great adoration towards Pepeelika, the Brahmin girl, as she had the courage to marry a Muslim guy, Aijaz, inspite of all the patriarchal norms. Together they visited many places and temples. These visits made them great friends. They came close and understood each other very well. They shared common pain and suffering. This made them understand each other well. Thus they started to establish a new relationship which was totally against all patriarchal norms and condition, against Indian culture and tradition, that is, a lesbian relationship. Ashok Kumar narrates, Astha likes to have a break from dependence on others and proceeds on the path of full human status that poses in threat of Hemant and his male superiority. Although, she finds herself trapped between the pressure of the modern developing society and shackles of ancient biases she set out on her quest for a more meaningful life in her lesbian relationship. (Kumar, 134)

Unlike Hemant, Astha finds Pepeelika to be more caring and understanding. She got a kind of great solace in the arms of Pepeelika. Astha is caught in a dilemma- whether to stay with tradition or to enjoy herself without considering them. Astha told her husband that she was going on a pilgrimage to the Babri Masjid Mosque at Ayodhya. There she and Pepeelika enjoys time together.

Astha refused being close to Hemant as she found a condom in his bag one day. As he is indifferent towards her and shows no concern to her emotions, she is mentally detached from him. She found more time to spend with her new mate, Pepeelika. Unlike her husband, Pepeelika was more caring, loving and understanding towards Astha. Their relationship rebelled against man's attitude and his superiority by asserting their quest for freedom and self independence in a male dominated society. Thus, her association with Pepeelika gave a new turn to her quest for identity and self fulfillment. There arose a conflict between the roles of a wife, mother, daughter in law and that of a lover. Astha is also trapped in a dilemma between her obligation towards her family and her quest for freedom, whether she should stay back and be a dutiful wife and mother or should she run away for self independence. But tradition often pulls her back. She reminds herself of being a mother and a responsible wife. She realizes that a large part of her belongs to her family. She feels, "A willing body at night, a willing pair of hands and feet in the day and an obedient mouth were the necessary prerequisites of Hemant's wife" (2002, 231).

Pepeelika now becomes more possessive in the case of Astha. She wants her all alone. She always tries to separate Astha from her husband who neither appreciates nor understands her. She convinces Astha by saying that true love is something which should be felt by our heart. Love is not merely the union of two bodies but a union of souls, emotions and ideologies. She believes, "men were so pathetic, so fucked up themselves, they only understood the physical, and in this way she felt soothed" (209). When Hemant desires to have love making with his wife, she asks, "Do I have to give it just because you are my husband? Unless I feel close to you I can't – I'm not a sex object, you have others for that" (224). Astha wanted her husband as a friend with whom she could share her problems, as a husband whom she could rely on for comfort- thus he should be her life partner in every sense. But for Hemant, he wanted his wife as merely a person who obeys all his commands and does everything as he wishes her to do. He believes that a wife is for just ful- filling his sexual desires and his duty is only to observe her social needs.

Astha began to go to Pipee to satisfy her sexual needs. The lesbians enjoy themselves in their world of love. While Pepeelika forgets herself during sex, Astha takes a sweet revenge on her husband. Astha, having chosen a sexual identity willingly does not bother at all for moving away from her tradition and culture. Here Manju Kapur portrays women as more assertive and liberal in their attitude than the stereotyped Indian women portrayed in the earlier novels. Instead of passively suffering in the hands of her husband or lover, she now substantially asserts her rights through actions and not in words. She is now portrayed as a rebel who after suffering a lot, has turned against patriarchy. Astha feels her- self trapped between the pressure of modern developing society and shackles of ancient biases. She finds a more meaningful life in her lesbian relationship, where she finds a harmony between body and soul. Pipee becomes a motivator for Astha. She made her spell bound. As some magic is done on her, she acts according to Pipee's wishes. Pipee seems to be more understanding than Hemant. Moreover, she urges Astha to start a new relationship with her, "There was no aphrodisiac more powerful that's talking, no seduction more effective than curiosity." (218). It is Hemant's attitude towards Astha which made her an immoral wife rather than having a guilty consciousness of lesbian love.

Astha wants to keep both these relationships in a balanced way, keeping both side by side, without giving up either one of them. But as a wife and mother of two children, Astha tells Pipee:

> I love you, you know how much you meant to me, I try and prove it every moment we have together, but I can't abandon my family, I can't. May be I should not have looked for my happiness, but I can't help myself. I suppose you think I should not be in a relationship, but I had not foreseen…I am sorry I am not like you. (242)

On the other hand, when Astha gets all the comfort and affection from Pipee that she doesn't receive from Hemant, she thinks, "… if husband and wife are one person, then Pipee and she were even more so. She had shared parts of herself she had never shared before. She felt complete with her."(243). Thus Astha is now in a dilemma. But she can't leave Pipee as she is the one who gives her mental satisfaction. Through Pipee, Astha finds a satisfaction she did not get from Hemant. Whenever Pipee comes close to Astha, her heart begins to beat faster as a girl's heart beats when her lover touches her in a more passionate way. In the same way, she feels terrible if she could not meet Pepeelika. She "felt terrible the whole time". (230)

Lesbians are seen as the 'other' in many societies. They are considered as anomalies that do not fit into a heterosexual prototype. A lesbian is the rage of all women who are compressed into a state of destruction. When her needs are not satisfied, she becomes frustrated and pours her feelings in another form. These lead her to indulge herself in painful conflicts with people, behavior, situation and feelings around her and usually with herself.

Society allows women to enjoy her body and sexuality only in a heterosexual intimacy allowed by nature and also under marital cord. In her novels, Kapur presents the real life of a woman, who is bound by the rules of patriarchy has to efface her personality and surrender her very existence. She blames the socio cultural construct and comes to the conclusion that, "many facets of the relationship between her husband and herself reflected power than love."(233). More than love, man exerts his power over woman. This is what happens in conjugal life.

Astha feels herself disintegrated in every sense and wants to be reborn as a woman with all desires, aspirations, emotions, feelings and dreams. She sets on her quest for a more meaningful life in her lesbian relationship with Pepeelika, a widow. The female protagonist tries to break down the shackles of convention and challenges the heterosexual relationship which have degraded and marginalized lesbianism or homosexuality. She realizes herself as a faithless wife and accepts the miseries that follow her life. But she finds self satisfied in her relationship with Pipeelika. She defends herself through her feelings. "

Astha being fed up with disintegration of her body, wants to reinvent herself as a human being and wants to be reborn as a woman with all her desires, aspirations, emotions, feelings and dreams and sets on her quest for a more meaningful life in her relationship with Pepeelika, a widow. Astha, sometimes being a rebel, often rejects the family values and the rules she was to obey in her patriarchal society. She was brave enough to challenge the heterosexual power by indulging herself in much invalidated homosexuality or lesbianism. In this larger mainstream heterosexual world, the lesbians create a world of their own. This creates a critical reversal in the subject position. In the moments they spend together, they are no longer wives, daughters, mothers or any property which belonged to the patriarchal world, in which they live, but mere individuals, who enjoy their time together forgetting everyone and everything around them, the sole owner of their own bodies.

Pipee goes to US for her Ph.D. Astha becomes alienated again. But she gathers courage and goes to see her off at the airport. After seeing Pipeelika at the airport, Astha returns home. As she feels tired, she goes to sleep. Outwardly she looks the same but mentally she has changed a lot.

6

Conclusion

On assessing Manju Kapur's literary achievement, it becomes evident that she can be rightly called an Indian feminist writer. She is a realistic writer who thinks of emancipation of Indian woman only within Indian socio-cultural values. She never wants her protagonists to be 'super woman' who exceeds all the limits of Indian values. But she creates the concept of New Woman in them by providing them education. It must be through this education that Indian woman should think freely and independently. This leads to their emancipation in the right sense. That is what Manju Kapur portrays through her protagonists. They want to enjoy equal status with men in their society. For this, they find their own space in the society by becoming economically emancipated. Different from the real New Woman, Indian woman always values her family and motherhood. She can never think of liberation from her family. Manju Kapur always upholds feminism which suits Indian culture and tradition. Thus she also portrays that if a woman tries to transgress the limits of Indian culture, she never feels contended and becomes a failure in her life. Thus she can truly be called an Indian feminist writer in all its sense.

When we analyse the women protagonists in Manju Kapur's novels, we can find a progressive and conspicuous change with regard to their forward views against the traditional values which mark the modernity of their outlook. Through her novels, she has given voice to the voiceless.

Though a feminist and dreams the concept of a 'new woman' in her novels, deeply analyzing her novels, we can find that there is a moral underlying her novels. That is, for a happy married life, husband and wife should be faithful to each other. Extra marital relationships never give fulfillment in one's life. As a feminist who raises her voice for liberation of women, she wants Indian women to follow the culture of India. Through her novels, she has proved that any Indian woman who tries to cross the limits of Indian culture shall face the consequences in her life. India has a culture of her own and thus Indian women too. They should never defile their motherland. Within the limits of Indian culture, one shall gain one's freedom. Manju Kapur's feminism never goes beyond the limits of Indian culture. A woman should enjoy her rights. She could even demand her rights if denied. She should no more be considered a puppet in the hands of her husband or in-laws. Patriarchy should not stand against her wishes for development. She should have the right to education and freedom of speech. She should have the right to express her ideas. She should be treated as equal with her husband. True liberation of women is possible only when our over-all attitude is changed.

Manju Kapur wants Indian women to leave behind the old age tradition and fight for a better future. Her characters are examples of her concept of new Indian women. But through her novels, she gives a moral lesson that in India, every woman should follow a culture. The influence of Western culture to a certain extent is good, but marriage, a sacred institution, should not be spoiled by engaging in extra marital or any other perversions.

In Vedic age, women were given the status of goddess and it is believed that from their Shakthi emanated the male strength. The Vedas emphasize that women enjoyed a reasonably high position during the Vedic period. Two great epics of Hinduism, namely *Ramayana* and *Mahabharata* portray women in a good light. In Indian culture, the word which denotes strength and power is feminine that is, *Shakthi,* and all male power is derived from this feminine. This was the figure of women in Indian society. She was worshipped like a goddess- the incarnation of Devi Durga, the goddess of power. Then why women in today's society degrades

Every woman should be educated. She should raise her voice when her genuine rights are denied. She should fight for her rights. Every woman should be educated and she should be treated equally and equal opportunities should be given to her. But as a woman, she has some responsibilities. She should be a good wife and a mother. She should love her husband and children and do her duties. She should give prime importance to her family. Every woman is a mother. A mother has some responsibilities to her children. The husband and wife who live in harmony will get peace and satisfaction in their lives. This is what Indian culture demands. Any woman or man who crosses the limits can never find satisfaction in their lives. If one craves for satisfaction through extramarital relations, one could never enjoy a peaceful life. Extramarital relationships may give one pleasure, but it is short lived. One feels guilty in one's relations. One should be faithful to his or her family.

Throughout her novels, she has portrayed a wide variety of women characters, all from Indian middle class family. In her debut novel, *Difficult Daughters,* we come across women from three generations. Virmati's mother, a woman of old generation, is an example of a woman who supports patriarchy and who abides the rules generated by patriarchy. Same is the case with Ganga, Harish's first wife and Kishori Devi, his mother. Ida, daughter of Virmati, though divorced, keeps an identity of her own.we can see the same picture of a new woman in Shakuntala, Virmati's cousin. She is both educated and cultured. Though, once Virmati adored Shakuntala, and wanted to lead a life like hers, she couldn't follow Shakuntala in her morality. Ida and Shakuntala are images of new woman, whom India seeks today. But Virmati, who tried to move away from Indian culture, had to pay for her actions.

The second novel *The Immigrant* presents Nina, who is portrayed as an immigrant, tries to move away from Indian culture and becomes merely a puppet in the hands of three men. In the college, her first lover, Rahul takes away her virginity, her second man Ananda, her husband, uses her just as a timepass, while he involves in sex with other white women. After getting a job of a librarian, she meets Anton. Anton molests teases, makes love and finally rapes Nina. Nina herself is so much confused about her present condition. She is not able to share her feelings with anybody and suffers mentally.

Going through her third novel *Home*, Nisha is the protagonist and she is a traditionally brought up girl. Her mother Sona was a typical Indian mother who wanted her daughter to be grown according to the rules of patriarchy. Nisha is educated and is bold enough to face all the hurdles of life. But she never moves away from chastity. She also fights for her noble rights. In the end, we can see that Nisha leads a happy life with her husband and two children.

In her fourth novel, *A Married Woman*, the protagonist, Astha involves in lesbian relationship, seeking revenge on her husband. In the end, we can see that, neither has she succeeded in her life, nor she got inner peace. Breaking all the shackles and moving against the society, she tried to live a free life of her own. She tried to emerge as a new woman but she proved herself that she is not a new woman whom India needs.

The fifth novel *Custody* too portrays Shagun, who involves in extra marital relation with her husband's boss. The custody of her children is the central theme of the novel. But Shagun fails in gaining her children's love. Her daughter loves her father and goes with him. She accepts and loves Ishitha, her step mother. But Arjun, Shagun's son, can't accept his new father and moves to US. Thus Shagun loses her children, for whom she fought for.

Nisha, Ida and Shakuntala can be called the new women whom India needs in today's society. if a woman is not given equal rights with that of a man, why should she opt infidilty as the weapon of revenge? In a country like India, where women are treated like goddess, a woman instead of finding other relations to pacify her emotions, she should stay bold and fight for her rights. She should stand alone in this patriarchal society and achieve her goals through noble deeds. This is the 'new woman' whom everyone adores. She should be a role model for other women. This is the new woman in India's dream. Manju Kapur always wants a new woman who suits the culture of India. She can be truly called a post colonial Indian feminist writer.

Works Cited

Beauvoir Simone De *The Second Sex* Trans and ed. H.M.Parshley New York: Vintage Books 1989.

Kumar, Ashok. *Social Web and Cry of the Self: A Critical Analysis of Manju Kapur's A Married Woman.* Prasad, Amarnath. *New Lights on Indian Women novelists in English* Vol.4. New Delhi: Sarup and Sons, 2008.

Kapur, Manju. *Difficult Daughters.* New Delhi: Penguin, 1998.

-----------------. *A Married Woman.* New Delhi: India Ink, 2002.

----------------. *Home.* New Delhi: Random Books, 2006.

----------------. *The Immigrant.* New Delhi: Random House, 2008.

----------------. Custody. New Delhi: Random House, India, 2011.

Kumar, Gajendra. *Indian English Literature: A New Perspective.* New Delhi: Sarup and Sons, 2001

Swami, Indu. *The Woman Question in the selected novels of Nayantara Sahgal,Manju Kapur and Arundhathi Roy.* New Delhi: Sarup Book Publishers, 2009.

Varughese Dawson E. *Reading New India: Post Millennial Indian Fiction in English.* London: Bloomsburry publications, 2013. Kindle edition